GLOW

SELF-CARE POETRY FOR THE SOUL

An Anthology

Cover Art Copyright © 2023 by Indie Earth Publishing x Gloria Star
Illustrations Copyright © 2023 by Lashmit Alcalá

Edited by Flor Ana Mireles

1st Edition | 01
Paperback ISBN: 979-8-9880379-3-4

First Published June 2023

For inquiries and bulk orders, please email:
indieearthpublishinghouse@gmail.com

Indie Earth Publishing Inc.
| Miami, FL |

INDIE EARTH
PUBLISHING

Glow: Self-Care Poetry for the Soul

An Anthology

"WITHIN YOU,

THERE IS

A STILLNESS AND A

SANCTUARY

TO WHICH YOU CAN

RETREAT

AT ANY TIME

AND BE YOURSELF."

-- HERMAN HESSE

Poems

Poems

Poems

HERE BEGINS A JOURNEY OF SELF-CARE

Making Room For More
Tiffiny Rose Allen

The moon told me not to worry anymore.
The moon told me to make room—

I feel like I'm saying goodbye to the poet that I used to be
& I'm making room for more.

My self-love speaks to me.
It says, *Honey, baby,*
it's alright to stay,
it's okay,
you don't need the other things anyway,
not when you're right here home with me.

Please,
I have outgrown this name.
Let me find another that speaks to me.

Let me sit amongst the stars & swirl the planets
in a way that makes it all okay.

To The Person Who Taught Me To Think In Cursive, I'm Sorry I Miss You
Jake Price

A garden full of daylilies,
only daylilies.

I water them with ice sculptures I leave to melt inside the greenhouse.
I like to think the flowers see a metaphor in it,
& are not just sitting there with their petal tongues hanging, waiting
for a drip, a drop of meaning.

After they bloom, I dehead them like you're supposed to so they can
blossom again in the fall.

I showed you the garden once, & the stream behind it, & the field between the garden & the stream, & the foxglove that grew along the
side of the greenhouse, & I melted in front of the daylilies, their petal
tongues hanging, waiting for a drip, a drop of meaning.

Song of the River Trail
Cortney Casey

Remember this
when the days are dark & lightless
& the color has drained from the world again:
How dappled sunlight filtered
through the swaying leaves.
How red-winged blackbirds trilled,
scarlet epaulets flashing.
How baby rabbits ran you home along the trail
like tiny marathon pacers.
How deer stepped lightly across the river,
as graceful as dancers.
How dragonflies skipped across the water
like shimmering stones.
How sandpipers chided onlookers
as they scooted across the shoreline.
How twanging bullfrogs
bellyflopped into the lake.
How mallards turned vertical
seeking underwater treasures.
How geese necks shimmered
like black velvet in the river's reflection.
How long-pedaled purple coneflowers
reached hopefully for the sun
& pink hibiscuses unfurled,
flaring for a single day of brilliant life.
How you walked in the river & tried to decide
whether light through trees or on water was more exquisite.
How you wanted to swim instead of drown.
How time seemed endless and full of promise.
The days of light don't last forever,
but neither do the days of darkness.
Remember this.

Love
Pooja Gudka

It is not enough
to love one another,
first, we must love
ourselves.
Nourish our soul,
cherish ourselves,
as much as we do others.

At My Core
Veronica Szymankiewicz

The original me with default settings has been reset,
complete with a new mindset you'd do well to respect.
I've pieced myself back together again
with parts you may not recognize with your unsophisticated eyes.
Few can truly handle the intensity at my core,
as I try to harness the power raging within, evermore.
I was once broken, yet I do not need to be repaired.
Every crack in me has birthed an integral facet
of the woman I was meant to become,
all sharing space together & acting as one.
Inside me a fearless warrior resides,
I am a wounded healer
who takes on the pain of others willingly, until it subsides.
I am a poet who bleeds words in unconscious streams,
splattering thoughts & feelings like a crime scene.
I am a dreamer of fantastically impossible dreams
while dancing happily amongst glittering moonbeams.
I am a girl who sees beauty unseen,
by those who have become walking, talking & unfeeling machines.
I am a lover who will level the whole world down to the ground
for those she loves beyond human extremes.
I am a lioness that roars, refusing to be tamed by base & tiresome
regimes.
I am a vessel of infinite magic & divine light that flows & gleams,
my core, far more intricately complex than it outwardly seems.

Therapy
Nicole Smith

I'm a different person
than I was a few days ago.
I've molted the old version,
sloughing off bits as I go.
Growing, blooming, changing, evolving
finding footing in my new reality.
Discovering day by day
who I'm supposed to be.

Small Boobs
Annie Vazquez

When you told me you preferred big boobs
over my two small vanilla scoops
with cherries on top,
I felt the door to my heart slam
shut
& the pain of not being desirable
kick me in the stomach.

You said you'd pay for breast implants
& I wondered why you were okay with
seeing me on an operating table,
hooked to an oxygen tank,
scalpels & knives slitting me open
as if double As were a disease
you were saving me from.

I thought you loved nature?
Doesn't that mean loving
what's natural on a woman, too?

How could you ever ask me
to trade the beauty of my small
majestic snowy white hills
for two plastic pouches
molded to be mountains
just so you could feel
like you reached new heights?

Lack of self-love is poison
when you feel the need to ask a woman
to sacrifice the architectural wonder she is
for something less.

Love You For You
Courtney Forcefield

You do not have to turn yourself into someone else in order to be accepted.

Where did you learn this art, shape-shifting?
Was it from your own mother? Or from father culture?

Where did you learn to abandon your Self in the hopes that someone else might love you more...

when you have everything you need inside of you to love yourself exactly as you are?

Take off the mask & let yourself be.
Let yourself be seen for who you truly are.

I promise you can find a way to love you for who you truly are.

Eulogy
Stephanie Hawkins

"They love me, they love me not."
If only I had known I never had a shot.

A shot at demeaning my worth?
As if he even had any girth.

I take it back as that was crude.
But after all you did say,
"This is nothing serious, dude."

Why do rules never apply to you?
 You quite literally fit the shoe.

The past is designed for things that don't last.
So don't make this a reason to fast.

In the act of losing them, we lose ourselves.
My trophies belong on the shelves.

"I love me, I love me not."
If only I had known I've always had a shot.

Eastern Wind
Renzo Del Castillo

The exuberance of youth drives boys headfirst into Ceto's kingdom,
engulfed in Turquoise rhythms until only experience emerges,
dripping regret. Here is where you'll find me. Sitting on the sand.
Watching the waves' tenacity... waiting for you.
I trace the cracks on my inner lip with your tongue, admiring the
narcissism of grief & the expanse of my own ego for thinking I got to
decide when I was finished mourning the trips I took into the thrilling
unknown for the feel of your collarbone.
I sit here, above the sand of eroded Septembers, waiting for you. To tell
you that I am no longer seeking because there is nothing I lack. Instead
I explore, traveling the world as I'm able while different cities embrace
me, whispering their poetry in both ears.
I owe nothing & am owed nothing. I give what I want to give & receive
what I wish to receive. This is the gift life has for me & the lesson I
couldn't learn while I labored for your love: the world is chaos &
expectations will kill you. Make your own way.
I wait for you, beneath the breeze, in gratitude for all that you were,
for a moment, shaping the man I am & am becoming. I wait to tell you
what I've learned: that you are enough, that you are beloved, & that I
no longer wait for you.

Inner Loving Parent
Leigh Anne Hanigan

Dear loving parent,
　be with me as I struggle,
　embolden me when I feel fear,
　embrace me when I feel unlovable,
　reassure me when I feel I'm not enough,
　stay by my side when I feel I don't belong,
　show me warmth when I feel anxious,
　show me grace when I'm indecisive or make the wrong choice,
　be shocked when I question my existence,
　hold my hand & listen when I feel unimportant,
　be gentle and comfort me when I feel shame,
　be fiercely defensive of me when I don't feel my value,
　shower me with humor & playfulness,
　remind me that I am right where I should be & that everything I
feel is normal,
　　but it is not all to be believed,
　reiterate that I am not my thoughts,
　help me surrender so that I can release my false core beliefs.

Remember, You Created This For You
Courtney Forcefield

Remember,
there were days when you dreamt about
what it would be like to be where you are now.

Remember,
there were nights when you wondered
what it would feel like to feel what you're feeling now.

Remember,
there were moments when you questioned
if you would ever get here.

Remember
& give thanks for those past versions of you
that believed in you.
Those past versions of you
that betted on you
so you could be here *now*.

Count Me Out

Jade Baas

I wonder if the sun daydreams
about better times,
because maybe the throne in the sky
is not all the crown brags it to be.

Meditated in mother nature's embrace,
the warm soleil,
i have love in the sun;
love in the sky,
love to the loved ones in my mind,
love to water,
love to the trees,
love to flowers,
love to the leaves,
i love thy self.
This year, you better one yourself.
If you didn't learn to,
forgive me for
my need to forgive myself,
then, dawg,
i love when you count me out,
i love when you count me out,
i love when you count me out,
fuck it up, fucking it up, fucking it up.

I need you in person with me,
because memories are becoming nothing.
I'm aging, but I'm not growing.

You show me that you're here,
a purple butterfly to prove you're near.
I feel you only in the tears,

I'm trying to be the murder to fear.
There's a loss in every year,
but the strength in weakness
makes the vision more clear
& I just want to prove to all that left
I found a love that won't disappear.
I never needed you
or your pretend to care.
Sincerely, my dear.

Self-Preservation
Nicole Menzzasalma

The only time
you are truly
alone
is when
you
abandon
yourself.

Healing

self healing isn't straightforward
triggers lay enveloped
in corners of the subconscious
shadow work to heal
the inner child
the protector
the forgotten

Growing up
Just a mentally ill girl
trying to adult
in a world of
judgment and bullshit.
Loving that defenseless
little girl locked inside.
Telling her over and over
you can do it, it will all
be okay.
The universe has
bigger plans for you.

Reflections
Azure Hall

Oh, how I long to look upon myself as I once did, with soft eyes that are fully mine. To shed their scales that have grown brittle with exposure.

To again be led by the murmuring sound of cave waters that spread into a liquid plain & promise absolute acceptance.

I don't know when I first began to distinguish between water & sky & self, but that undifferentiated world feels lost to me.

It has been years since I laid down on that green bank & found a gleaming, watery shape that peered lovingly back at me. This crystalline likeness never questioned her place in the family of things, nor mine. She moved with the ripples & twinkled in the sunlight, owning them as parts of herself. But rather than hold onto her innate belonging, I left that familiar figure behind.

Despite the kind looks that shone up from the water, what else could I do but stand & follow straight where she could not go?

I was invisibly led to a world where I see myself through the gaze of another who is less fair, less soft, less mild than my reflection. This intended individual solace of fellowship has stripped me of the autonomy that led me to the lake in the first place.

Through these new eyes, looking upon myself with love feels like vain desire. My pool of pleasure has turned to salt tears. When I find myself out & bathing now, it is not that smiling mirror image that my eyes seek out for reassurance.

They are instead cast up & around, scanning for other eyes on me.

They are cast inward, reminding me to pull my belly closer to my spine

& sit straight to prevent it from folding.

They are cast down at my feet, should I begin to enjoy the attention too much, forgetting my humility.

I can no longer see myself in innocence.

I am under the constant assault of awareness that the shape is my own.

I ripped it from the surrounding context of connection & outlined its borders in a violent red.

I feel the amount of space it takes up in the world & long to shrink it down to something more manageable.

I search it for wrinkles & silver hairs, any reflective surface weaponized.

I blame it for not fitting into clothes that are too small to contain its supple wonder.

I punish it like a disobedient child with missed meals & cruel words that cut to the bone.

The bare skin that sparkled so stunningly turned indecent upon further examination.

The laughter that echoed from the shores sounds hollow & wholly too loud.

I am assured that I will live a long life, provided that I don't discover myself. Should I stay too long at the water's edge, I am likely to grow frail & consumed with my own image. But lately, the divine voice that first broke my silent self-contemplation has begun to grate like grinding teeth.

The repetition of its constant criticisms & reminders to pose for invisible cameras no longer hold my attention as they once did. My mind wanders from them & I find myself drawn to more interesting topics of conversation.

So, too am I often caught unawares by the sudden appearance of something that vaguely resembles the face I found in the water so many years ago. Despite the empty echoes of encircling hands that aim to drown her out, she appears peripherally.

I have seen her smiling in shop windows as I stroll through the city with my sisters.

She peers out at me through the wide eyes of my daughter that look up to me as we read books in bed.

I hear the lapping of her waves in laughter that sometimes escapes from me unbridled.

She whispers gentle reminders of the magic of our shared shape, of its elegant endurance.

As I bend to look, she bends just opposite. Still, I start back from her & she from me. Time has made us nearly strangers.

But should I return, pleased, she will be waiting with answering looks of sympathy & love; waiting with forgiveness & the cool caress of cave water.

Her Treasures From Within
Thuy Nguyen

She was a giver. They, the taker.
She gave so much of what is of intangible value.
They did not see her value, but rather saw their advantage.

She offered her hand, but they claimed it was too small.
She offered her heart, but it was not love they were seeking.
She offered her soul, to which they claimed as their own.
She offered her light, but they consumed it with their own darkness.
She offered her authenticity, but they mocked it to cast her aside.
She offered her truth, but they desired to stay veiled in their illusion.
She offered many opportunities to say yes, until she was too depleted
to say no.

What they did not value,
she woke to determine her own worth from within.
She realized that what they rejected
was the Universe's loving way to be protected.
& for this, she continued
to pour her value into those who had the eyes to see.
As she filled her well from within,
so she poured her endless overflow upon those who thirsted.
For then, she offered to those who valued every drop of water.

My Before & After
Renee Lynn Furlow

Other worldly experiences,

a past that is painful.

This is my before.

Emotions ran high—

pain, fears, sadness,

a broken soul

coming to a conclusion—

I knew I had to break the cycle.

So I stood up.

I broke the mold,

& my after became

so bright & inspirational.

The ability to stride

into a life that was my own—

the strength it took—

I had to find my brave,

& I did.

I really did that.

When Are You Going Home?
Jaime Lam

A girl made of glass
can reside in poetry. A question
mark, a home—cocoon into
the curve. Em-dashes make
bed frames, & voltas
serve wake up
calls.

Maybe
she'll even learn
to erode, tucked inside a
quatrain. All that breakage
softening under streaming lyric
until she lives all
over again.

Thunder Thighs
Annie Vazquez

You called me thunder thighs
like it was a bad thing to
to walk into rooms loudly with my
God-given body.

Thunder thighs.
Oh me, oh my.
Why should I apologize for my curves
that move from side to side like a
delicious disco beat?

Thunder thighs.
Oh me, oh my.
Honey, I wasn't made
to squeeze into a certain size
or a "goal" weight
or deprive myself from enjoying life.
I did that far too long when

you convinced me to
hate these thighs.

Thunder thighs.
Oh me, oh my.
I am no longer a hushed rainstorm.
I'm a make-the-ground-shake
with confidence
thunderstorm
here to leave you thunderstruck.

Oh me, oh my.

This Sad Part Of Me, I Love Him Too
Courtney Forcefield

If I'm feeling sad, there must be some part of me that wants to feel sad. Otherwise, why would I do it?

The excuse, "You can't help the way you feel," just doesn't fly here. Because I know how powerful we all are & I know I'm capable of anything, least of all changing the way I feel.

So I will get to know this being within me that wants to be sad & discover why he wants to be sad & enjoy the sadness with him.

Self-Love Is A Prayer To The Ocean
Ashley Lilly

Self-love is a prayer to the ocean.
     Cleanse me, heal me, help me go
with the flow
     of cool, glistening waves,
        their salty drops whispering,
  'It's okay to cry;'
     the mysteries of the sea floor
singing a lullaby about
          hidden
    treasures.

  Self-love
  is a meadow,
bursting with flowers
  in every color.
   A rainbow
    that
    sways
     in
     the
    wind.
   Rosebuds
    waiting
    with
   patience
   &
    grace
    to
  b l o o m.

Empty From Within
Alshaad Kara

You broke the shell
of my mind,
emptying my dreams
from within.

My whole world fell apart
because of you.

However,
the self-care journey
was unleashed,
to remedy the damage
I suffered.

It was the start
of my own cure,
to take care
of my core.

Untitled
Bushra Ali

As the daylight flickers
on my darkest days,
when the room is a cage
captivating me in an ugly way,
they say let it be; it is what it is.
We can't change everything,
though little do they know,
it's themselves they can't change.
According to their laws,
mental health can be sold;
not the preserved money and gold.
What they didn't know is,
I might be scared at mind, but not at heart.

When I Dance With Her
Aphrodite's Devotee

When I dance with Her,
our feet follow,

skipping through
terrains of sorrow,

leaving red anemones behind;
leading the way to my
Infinite Divine.

I ask Her,
what do you do, child,
to feel so alive?
She replies with my gaze:

I am simply here,

nowhere near or far.

Always. Just. Here.

To Watch Flower Petals Fall
Amelie Honeysuckle

I let the flower pedals fall
one
by
one
as they tiptoe their way to the floor.

I sit
bathing in the sun,
cooking away in the tender rays.
My freckles begin to peak out;
they creep to the surface.
I breathe in slowly,
I let the air fill my lungs,
then I shoot up one more breath
& let it out.

Away I float,
the world around me
finally in harmony.
I spin around,
a full 180
& glare at myself.
I am raw,
I am powerful,
I am brave,
I am kind,
I am alive.

I let the world soak on my freshly washed skin,
bathing once again in the rays
but with full awareness & control.
I am thankful,

& I stand mindfully
as I watch the pedals fall
one
by
one
as I become completely undone.

Ever-Unfolding Rose
A. W. Jones

Self-love is a seed already within you;
allow it to sink into your soul
& plant itself there.
Shelter it with tenderness.
Nurture it with sensitivity.
Nourish it with compassion.
Let it take root & bloom in patience,
to unfurl its beauty in the wisdom
of its own timing,
& you will find it to be
an ever-unfolding rose.

Total Hysterectomy
Cara Morgan

Take this—my body, my blood.
Let me be rid of it.
This organ, bitter & bruised. Sick & afraid.

No more.

Cut her from me carefully & I will birth her.
A dying babe.
An alien infested.

When I wake, I'll see her in pictures & know it is done.
They'll say it's over, but it's only beginning.
A new kind of wholeness. Selfhood.

I will heal my wounds as my heart—
Slowly, thoughtfully, & with soup.
Shedding what I've outgrown,
freeing up room to dance.

I will live in my body uninterrupted.

Joyous & free.

It's Not That I Don't Love Myself
Ashley Lilly

It's not that I don't love myself,
but I don't always love life.

Darkness, the void, invisible scars,
racing heart, sweaty palms, fight or freeze

or flight.
I don't always want to stay.

I'm tethered to the trees, the moon, the sun,
but the space between me and the things I love

turns to dust.
How do you feel loved

when your brain is lost in the mud
& your heart is somewhere in outer space?

Sometimes, self-love
is opening your arms

to let the sky wrap you up in a hug.
She'll tell you, *The rains will come.*

She'll tell you,
& so will the sun.

Phoenix Reborn
Veronica Szymankiewicz

Don't mind the ashes that flutter about
as I walk steadfast towards my fate,
for I was burned in the unrelenting, searing fires of sorrow & hate.
A Phoenix reborn, not a second too late...
Now watch while I alchemize & create
pure magic from my soul that you'll never again
be able to confiscate or desecrate.
Feathered wings unfurling as I begin to elevate,
I'm done with those who only seek to manipulate & subjugate.
Test me & I'll spit out the very flames used on me
in failed attempts to annihilate.
Never underestimate the ferocity of a woman
with nothing left to lose as she realizes
she was always meant for something great.

Phases
John Queor

Every few months,
I buy a bouquet
of flowers to sit
on my dining room table
until they die,
& then, I
bring them
to my bedroom.

I find beauty in both
phases of a flower's life;
fragrant & vibrant,
turning darker,
down turned.

The corners of my room
are decorated in dead
roses & sprigs of lavender,
a duality of romance & peace.
The perfect place to
fall in love with my own phases.

Don't Compromise
Vincent J. Hall II

Don't compromise
on yourself. You're
better than that.

Don't sacrifice your
time to please other
people. Not for a
minute.

Don't settle for anything
less than what you
deserve. You're
worth more.

I tell myself this
everyday. To remind
myself that the first
person to love me
each morning should
be *me*.

Eager For the Undergrowth
Renee Lynn Furlow

So much has held me back,

from the child struck down again & again

to the young adult trapped in a situation

that I could not possibly get out of.

Deciding to take back my life one day

created a deep sense of eagerness

to grow, not only on the surface,

but to dig deep & allow the darkness

to be a gift as well as the light.

The undergrowth is the root

propelling me up for greatness.

A Cure For Loneliness
Flor Ana

The first thing you need
is a mountain of self-love,
& I know the climb
can be steep,
but I promise you
the view is worth it.

Next, be sure to get
an ocean of music
& let the rhythms & waves
wash away
the worries of the day.

The third thing you need
is a sky full of stars,
to remind you that we're all
just stardust
& you can never be lonely
when you're a star yourself.

The last remedy necessary
is a universe of love,
for everything & everyone.
Because the universe always
has your back & exists
for just your love.

Don't Forget To Breathe
Jaime Lam

There will be more
somedays, darling. Tomorrow
might have rain, &
won't that be incredible?

Remember you are never too old
to rewrite yourself—I know
you mourn all lost
yesterdays.

Do you realize dawn
can't help but come?
How lucky you are—
he cannot take everything.

Untitled
Kachay A. Bell

Happiness
has reached my heart
& my, oh my,
is it a wonderful feeling.
The days look brighter,
the smiles are wider
& the skin glows
like it never has before.
Happiness
has filled my heart
& my, oh my,
it sure feels good.

Shampoo, & Unconditionally
John Queor

Eucalyptus drops
at the base of my tub,
helping to clear my mind.
You have no idea
how cluttered I've become .

I turn the water on,
wisps of steam wet my face,
caressing my contours like a hug,
& I think about being held.
& I think about being released.

I lather the shampoo between my palms.
I cover every single strand in soap,
focusing the product into the roots.
I force all the dark thoughts to flee,
to leave me confident & clean.
& then, I condition.
I work on loving myself unconditionally...

Waiting Ward
Alshaad Kara

I am in an open world,
but you in a closed ward.

The contrast is,
I feel so empty,
whereas
you feel empathetic,

yet your absence
has been maddeningly sad.

Though I know
you will get better,
I miss you
& pray for your recovery.

Breathe
Kendall Hope

Smile sweetly
as the thunder rolls over your bones
& mellows out through the fog of your heart.

Light a candle
in the dark
as the fire builds inside your brain
& dissipates from a gentle rain.

Close your eyes
as the sound of your breath rolls into your chest,
until there is no worry left.

Rebellion
Veronica Szymankiewicz

Lost in an endless sea of uniformity,
rebellion rises within against the forced conformity.
Who would want to continue living this absurdity for the rest of
eternity?
Who cares how one is perceived externally,
when the fires of individuality rage internally?
Considered perversity to purposely covet diversity,
shunned & made to feel like an abhorrent deformity.
She began her rise wordlessly,
leaving behind the facade of normalcy.
Covered in red war paint, she stood alone controversially
& bore the crushing enormity of these affairs perfectly.
No longer fearing uncertainty,
she fought fervently & drank in her new world thirstily.
She was always meant to lead the insurgency,
blossoming into herself gorgeously...
A visual reminder to always live one's truth unapologetically &
unreservedly.

A Heart In Everything
Taya Boyles

In 1,000 of the multiverses,
there is a version of the Canary Islands
that houses an assortment of dragon trees

& chamomile with snow petals,
Arnica with sun bulbs all lined
up like soldiers at attention.

There is everlasting sunlight.

You have no part in this beauty,

but it is in existence.

Just like a version of you that is flourishing
in rose-gold, tending to the strawberries
ripening to
feed thousands,
where you are at peace.

You have no part in this beauty,

but it is in existence,
just like you.

Watering Your Roots
Thuy Nguyen

It's that kind of day, where dark clouds loom overhead, & you are achy, exhausted & the only way is rolling out of bed.

Have your cry, but go on.

The tasks are insurmountable, reaching up to the sky. However do you even begin to reach that high?

Have your cry, but go on.

The world beats down upon your shoulders, pebbles are placed atop your heap & wears you down in the burdens as heavy as boulders.

My dear, have your cry, but go on.

You dodge the stones they throw while watching you from afar bearing such heavy weights; their efforts to trample you down to stay low in hates.

Have your cry, but now, look up.

The beauty of being trampled on to such a low makes way for you to cultivate the inner strength to grow—upwards, despite blow after blow.

Have your cry, but now, look down.

All your tears wept, seeped into the soil below to water your roots deep, nourishing your seeds to soon sow.

Cry no more, & see with purified eyes all that you have become.

You can only look down at the soil that kept you grounded through all of those storms—
because you bloomed into the sturdy tree that you now are by continually standing tall against the norms.

You have bloomed, my dear, from every tear shed into the well that nourished your soul to become so deeply rooted.

So yes, go on & have your cry, but now from your deep inner well—of joy, peace, & abundance derived from such a season of hell.

May we all become transformed through our hellfires—for this makes way for our inner phoenixes to rise from the ashes.

Brothers
Renzo Del Castillo

Little brother, disregard your constraints. You find beauty in life when you ignore the ticking clock. Time is ongoing, incomplete, eternal. Experience the passage of time; honor it. We evolve between moments because we choose to. Use your time, give it value, live in the moment, choose a path from the infinite choices before you & close yourself off from the distraction of other paths. There is no other road but the one you're on.

Do not be ruled by the tyranny of "what if." Affirm the moment &, in doing so, affirm all of existence. Be lured by your senses. Build relationships. They're hard work, but it's work worth doing... There's an inherent romanticism in the amount of effort put forth to keep things going. When the old genre of romanticism can no longer sustain you, look for a new genre. You know you're in the right place at the right time when you meet the right person. Indulge in the sapiosexual experience of the enjoyment & sensuality of dialogue. Walk & talk with others as a response to death. Create.

Art changes as you change. Feel abandoned by its love in the moments between actions. People leave us, transforming excitement into longing & a desire to follow in the alchemy of meaning. The only meaning that matters is the meaning you create, not only in your identity but also in your identity in relation to others. Make the choices that determine who you are, without fear. All you have is now, little brother. All you will ever have is now.

My Hair
Vanessa 'Kaylyn Marie' Gallegos

My hair;
my mom brushing my hair.
Her mom hitting her with a brush;
we have to be tough.
Resilient,
my hair has never been,
but when I started to tend to it
& myself,
I started to see some of my Native American self.
It got long, you see.
When I braid it
& they tell me I look like Pocahontas,
it's a cherished thing to me,
but used to be something I ran from,
not wanting to accept parts of me,
also told I wasn't really enough
of something to claim it.
Like being Spanish, if you can't speak it.
Sometimes people put us into categories
before we even know ourselves,
way before they find themselves.
& even when we think we're past it,
it's on the shelves,
in the closet of our bodies,
the ones that hold on to every trauma
like a sick keepsake of someone obsessed
even when we're doing our best.
It's in my hair you'll see the test
of time.
Each gray hair I find
reminds me that I'm living this life.
My grandpa's hair went white early,

but he kept it styled so purty,
something so familiar to me.
My mom styling my grandmas hair before bingo,
the way my cousin braided my hair
toughencd me up,
taught me how,
for when they're not here,
I never really valued my hair.
I used to want it to be curlier, longer,
something some may see as stronger,
but as I cursed at it,
it recoiled in fear.
Love
was something my body could no longer hear.
All of my pain held there
in my hair,
in my body,
everywhere;
a Native American who never treasured their hair.
When it came to graduation,
a sash they wanted me to wear
to show my peers
my deepest fears,
imposter syndrome very clear
because they told me I wasn't one of them.
Or did I just hear that?
Because being mixed
causes my identity to feel like a trick.
I've been to the dances,
I've ate the food.
Why does it feel like there's always something I'm trying to prove?
To you and you,
because I don't know what to do.
When it comes to sharing my identity with you,
I've never known what to put down.

They don't let you pick two,
so Caucasian is what I'm used to,
but they kind of doubt it
when your name doesn't ring true.
Then, other Mexicans wonder why you can't speak two
languages with a name like that
& with a face like that.
We know it's something else.
Eventually, I had to choose myself,
every little part,
take those things off the shelf
& learn to love myself.
My mixed race may be confusing to you.
No, I won't ever sound or look like you might think,
but I also won't let it be me that shrinks.
I'll be me in every moment
because I'm resilient,
like every woman I come from,
like my hair that I leave undone.
Gray hairs woven in because I don't run;
I live for my ancestors now
& they're thriving.
Can't you tell?

The Self-Care Contract
Ashley Lilly

Eat the crisp apples & the leafy green salad,
but also enjoy chocolate cake & salty pretzels.

Sleep while the moonlight kisses your cheeks,
but also stay up late to laugh under the stars.

Move your body with walking, running, yoga & weights,
but also take time to lay down, to be still, to do nothing.

Close your eyes, breathe, listen, let go,
but also let your passions bring you to life.

Keep a few good friends close; it's all you need,
but also take time for you, your thoughts & the clouds.

Take care of yourself; this life is all you have,
but also cry, dance, twirl, fingerpaint; this life is all you have.

The Heart Of The Mind
Alshaad Kara

Listen to the talks of the mind,
concerning one's own self care,
before burning out.

But nothing shall replace
the heart that keeps caring
for oneself.

No painkillers
can kill the harsh words,

but being mentally strong
is what mirrors the mind
as a mental warrior.

A Quick Note To Krystal At The Cafe
Azure Hall

Gather up the scraps of you, my girl.
The battered & beaten golden rays,
the fragments
with their jagged edges.

Though the holding
may be painful,
though you will seep sweet crimson,
the healing will come.

Hold your shards close.
Grip them in a mighty fist.
Let the pain seep through the gaps
in your strong fingers.

& when,
finally,
you own the agony,
let go.

You may worry away
those sharp corners,
or one day, find all the ways
in which your angles fit perfectly inside.

On those bright mornings
when the sunlight peeks through
your remaining fissures, remember,
you are born in the breaking.

Survival Guide
Kelli Weldon

Push it away
or embrace it;
you can be the one
to decide.

A rooftop bar, a debut, twinkle lights hanging over you;
drink something hot,
pay for it with shiny coins.

Wrap yourself in something
soft and clean,
something that suits you,
a new beginning.

Flourishing In Solitude
Thuy Nguyen

To have no choice but to be alone, some may find it lonely.
It will be lonesome to wake up to oneself,
but she learned to greet the day by herself.
It will be lonesome to talk to oneself,
but she learned to speak her own thoughts to herself.
It will be lonesome to walk with oneself,
but she learned to stand up tall & move forward with herself.
It will be lonesome to sit with oneself,
but she learned to support her own back for herself.
It will be lonesome to eat with oneself,
but she learned to nourish body, mind, & soul—every part of herself.
It will be lonesome to cry with oneself,
but she learned to collect those tears & water the roots within herself.
It will be lonesome to fully dream for oneself,
but she learned to fully trust the aspirations set within herself.
It will be lonesome to sleep alone with oneself,
but she learned the warmth of her own skin in the nightly embrace of
herself.
Yes, it will be lonesome to be alone with oneself,
but she learned to embody the pure essence of herself.
In this solitude, she quietly found everyone she needed—herself
& she began to truly flourish.

Divine Feminine Energy
Kendall Hope

I am divine feminine energy.
I am masculine and magical, too.
My soul rules this body
& I mustn't act a fool.

I am divine feminine energy.
I am patient, gentle, & kind.
My heart loves deeply
& is nothing you can typically find.

I am divine feminine energy.
You cannot see through me,
but if you look close enough,
you will see me within.
A drop of sunshine
with the power for storms.
Plant me in the garden
& I will be home.

I am divine feminine energy.

(Self)Love Notes
Kristen Noelle Richards

I bought myself a dusty mason jar
from the thrift store on 19th & Uintah
just to fill it with everything
i have told my body not be, drove
10 hours to the grand canyon
to see the hate leap from its own ledge
& build itself wings.
A walk 5,000ft down
& I find myself falling in love
with all I tried to rid myself of.

Painting a picture from the bellies of leaves,
I let my body become an earth song.
Now, I am in Arizona, writing myself a million love notes
& hiding them in the folds of my skin,
every place I have tried to abandon.
So the next time I cannot see the beauty,
I will find the words that remind me
to love.

A Fragile Houseplant
Flor Ana

I've become a fragile houseplant,
hidden from the sun and thirsty for sunshowers.
I wish I could say it's by choice,
but the truth
is my mind is elsewhere,
vined & thorned
& sending its nutrients *elsewhere.*

I've become a fragile houseplant,
wilting under a frosted window.
I've lost my bloom
under sheets of linen,
petals wrinkled by
the passings of time,
smudged onto under-eyes of days-old mascara
as desert suns create mirages of the flower I could be.

I wish to drink the fruits of my labor better,
softer,
with a paintbrush in hand,
a cup of chai in the other, like the artists do.

Instead, I sit & think & think & think
& it never seems to end,
but *no.*

Today will be different.
Today there will be light
& I will sip the waters of the blessed trees to
refresh my dried & dying petals, my fallen leaves.
Because I am a marigold goddess & I will not
allow myself to wither like weeds.

Philautia
Renzo Del Castillo

You must move forward.
Take what's left of bike rides in September,
moonlit bonfires by the ocean, of her warm thighs before breakfast.
Take what's left & rebuild the frayed edges of your self-esteem
before they flutter away into the nothing you feed
whenever you pick at the scabbed flesh of your misplaced love.

You deserve more than you accept.

Please, learn this.
You'll blink and these years will join the others,
lost & forgotten, breathing dust in the caverns of the past.
Stop focusing on the size of your muscles & your body fat percentage,
cursing your genetics for making abs a seeming impossibility.
Your family doesn't have to struggle anymore; you've made it.

& if it all goes away, you will find a way... forward.

There's still life left to live,
to enjoy; moments to inhabit,
& affirmations to validate:
You are worthy. You are loved.
You are enough.

I Know Very Little About Nothing
MOZË

What do you know about nothing?
Literally sitting there, still, & doing no-thing.
It is one of the hardest things one can do.
I've been haunted by the thought of nothing
whilst simultaneously craving it,
addicted to hyper productivity
without even realizing it.
I was convinced that *nothing* equated to lazy,
& so I watched myself get past me.
I was convinced that I had to search,
doing things aimlessly for validation,
hoping it would mean
that I was worth something,
all at the expense of disregarding *nothing*.

What If?
Bushra Ali

We say that every night
welcomes a new day,
but what if we say the opposite?
What if we say that every bad day
has a good night to it?
What if we say every seemingly colorful day has a calming blue night
to it?
What if we say every happy moment
has a dark yet tranquil aftermath to it?
What if we say that every thing they
forcefully fed our brains doesn't define
us & neither does our life?
What if we say that being alone is
not a necessity, but a choice?
What if we say being disastrous is
incredibly fun sometimes?
What if we say there is joy in
ruining things sometimes?
What if we say the amount we feel
our emotions is immeasurable?
What if we say that there is no harm in spending some time in our
fictional world?
What if we say being dramatic is
sometimes what we need?
What if we say pouring out ourselves is
so much more than just embarrassing?
What if we decide to play along
within each other's boundaries?
What if we appreciate everything &
yet nothing to feel ourselves?
What if we dare to listen
a little more than we speak?

What if we accept the ones
who chose to hid themselves in poetry?
What if we say every bad story has
a marvellous ending to it?
What if we say the end is what makes it worth living?

I Am Allowing
Cece Rose Trezza

I am allowing myself to play.
I am allowing myself the energy & consideration to
paint,
sing,
laugh,
to explore & uncover stories deep within my mind
without burden,
without constraints.
Freely, like my inner child desired.

I am allowing myself to cry.
I am allowing myself to go with the wind of my emotions,
follow them to the deepest & darkest corners of my mind,
unafraid,
unscathed,
grieving what was lost,
appreciating what was gained
& giving myself the time & space I need to process & heal
until I am whole again.

I am allowing myself to hope.
I am allowing myself to believe in & pray for a better tomorrow, today.
To trust,
to imagine,
& find my way towards the life I want,
the life I will have & create,
watering my garden,
where desires manifest rapidly into reality.

I am allowing myself to be home.
I am allowing myself to be the safe space I always needed.
To be the person & place I run to when things are hard,

the rock that holds steady & weathers the storm,
providing shelter
to the thoughts,
emotions,
& feelings
that seek solace beneath.

I am allowing myself to trust.
I am allowing myself to be vulnerable,
aware that, although not everyone may hold my heart with such care,
the universe will never send me what I can't handle, grow, or bounce
back from.
I will never find myself in situations
which do not benefit me
& further my growth.

I am allowing myself to speak up.
I am allowing myself to say what is on my mind.
To choose who & what I give my energy to,
recognizing which situations benefit me
& which do not,
& leaving those which hurt or drain me, without hesitation.
For now I know
that energy
should always be an equal exchange.

I'm allowing myself to laugh.
I am allowing myself to find & focus on all the joy this world has to
offer,
recognizing the irony of life & falling in love with the universe's sense
of humor.
Focusing on the positive,
disregarding the negatives,
& embracing my role as cosmic jester.

I am allowing myself to breathe.
I am allowing myself the time & space to gather my composure
& find peace in my body,
treating it as a temple,
honoring it with words, thoughts, food, practices, & prayers,
letting myself inhale,
exhale,
expand,
contract,
& flow freely.

I am allowing myself to be courageous.
I am allowing myself to climb the tree of life,
towards the fruit of knowledge.
To take steps that scare every fiber of my being,
to say words that shake the concrete ground
& act in ways that allow others to do the same.

I am allowing myself to create.
I am allowing myself to let my essence flow freely in every room I
enter,
constructing worlds & stories
that my inner child can play in.
Creating for the sake of creating, for joy,
not for what I can produce.

I am allowing myself to heal.
I am allowing myself to understand what has hurt me
& work through the trial & tribulations,
becoming stronger & more self-aware with every blunder.
Recognizing that true growth is not linear,
is not easy,
but necessary,
&, with my persistence,
possible.

I am allowing myself to experience all that is.
I'm allowing myself to live freely,
passionately,
recklessly,
in the moment,
loving & embracing every high & low,
every struggle triumph,
thankful to have a life to do so.

I am allowing myself to be me.
I am allowing myself to be completely & entirely my own.
Free from restrictions & impositions,
embracing who & what I am,
becoming lost in the woods of my own mind.
Loving myself completely,
unconditionally,
for me.

Winds Of Change
Nicole Smith

I knew change was coming
by the way the winds blew.
Old lines of thinking,
their time was finally through.
I felt something stir
from deep within.
My journey of forgiveness & self-love
was about to begin.
Making healthy changes,
long overdue.
Casting off the old ways,
learning something new,
Look out for the new me;
she'll be making her debut.

Piano Lessons
Leigh Anne Hanigan

This morning,
she makes music,
fingers gliding across keys,
muscle memory guiding them along.
Recalling the lessons from decades earlier,
hand position, fingering, forte, pianissimo, andante,
struggling still to balance mechanics with the beauty of song.

But what are the new lessons here,
the ones that are overshadowing the actual act?
What does the piano know
that she hasn't paid close enough attention to?

The piano knows
that each hand must play its own part,
express itself individually,
with its own intricacies, complexity, & dynamics,
whether melody or harmony
so that together, the lines are a perfect complement to one another.

The piano knows
that differing tempos & dynamics,
are critical to the interest of the piece.
To the authenticity of its meaning,
to the way it helps the listener connect
so that they may experience a full range of emotions within.

The piano knows
that the beauty does not lie within the perfection,
but rather within the soul of the player.
The one who lets herself go, is carried by the music,
lost in its message, embraced by its insistence

so that she and the listener are transfixed, transported, transformed.

Lady On Fire
Aphrodite's Devotee

With passion,
manifesting
violet flames of
acceptance,
she walks her path
without fear of
burning down
her surroundings,

for she bares my name,
my face & my desire,
to be fully authentic
& loving of herself.

No matter what the whispers say.
No matter what transpires.

Crow
Johanna Hatch

Sweating & aching,
balanced on splayed palms
& too-soft triceps,

I push off the mat,
asking my fear to silence herself
for once.

& I cackle aloud,
because, for a moment,
I flew.

Pitching Pebbles
MOZË

I once thought
I could carry the world
within my mind.
Making a mountain
out of a molehill
became ritual.
I really believed
that disaster was all consuming.
Until I learned how to pitch pebbles on water, that is.
One small pebble could tread the river, lake—hell, even the ocean,
leaving ripples in its wake.
We are made up of mostly water,
& one good thought was all it would take.

Yes To Myself
Aphrodite's Devotee

Saying no to you
is saying yes to myself.

Saying no to you
is watering the roots,
firm in the ground of my will.

Saying no to you
fills me with peace,

for I am protector
of my being,
the duality of simply being,

& creating the space
to be with myself

feeling.

Sunrise Meditation
Diana Kurniawan

Suffused with spirals of thought.
Inside the vortex of my mind.
Unknown of the depth of them.
Only felt the shallow anxieties.

Looked on the mirror to reflect,
saw no reflection, only reaction.
The visual of manic on my skin,
the result of past asphyxiation.

Letting the tears fall was courage.
The bravery in the unrelenting.
The mastery of the persisting.
The divination to keep loving.

Emotions feast on the soul.
The best of us let it unwind,
not in action, but in poetry—
the triumph of morning glory.

Those Who Create Battlefields Out Of Rose Gardens
Taya Boyles

You grew up throwing knives & playing darts,
aiming higher for the red with your father,
lower for the bullseye with your mother,
& still missing when you made a mark on either side
of the board.
Don't fret, challenger.
You've taken the hardest step in
realizing the choice is between sage & stardust,
how long you're willing to burn,
and who for.

Autumn Nights
dsb.poetry

Rain falls
from gray skies
as I find myself
sitting across from
a woman, my love, or
best friends over
a cup of hot coffee,
notebook in front of me,
backpack of books
seated next to me,
no worries of work
to pierce my mind,
high on the passing time.

It's a vibe
saved solely for
the purpose of
pleasure in my mind—

a moment of
euphoria,
frozen in time

my Sunday best.

The Scientist & The Monster

A. J. Flora

I took my thread & scissors
& sewed myself together;
I placed myself from limb to limb
to make a better man.
I made each part painstakingly
& filled it with my love;
I kissed every stitch & let myself
revel in the act of creation.

But when I step out
& let the sun kiss me too,
I feel not the firm grasp of the sun,
not the gentle embrace of the moon.
I feel coldness of a stare,
the heat of their weapons & their torches
in their hands, in their hearts;
so even when they look away
the flames lick at me.

i fall apart,
my stitches grow tired & slack
& my limbs part with every step.
You can watch me,
held together by strings,
struggle in the light of day,
but I pray
please
look
away.

But I will drag myself back home
& I will mourn my art;

I will bring forth my love.
It seeps through the bones & the blood,
the muscle & the organs;
even when they spill out onto the pavement,
they are mine.

I was born to create,
to make & to love,
& I will always
put myself together again.

Untitled
MOZË

I am getting better,
I swear it.
This is what I repeat to myself,
scouring through posts & posts
about healing oneself.
It takes a couple seconds to post something,
reply sometimes relies on impulses
that too takes seconds.
We can dish out advice
when the point of reference is not us
& that can take seconds.
Healing, however,
that does not take seconds.
It takes years of self-abuse
& years of unwinding.
It takes years of confusion
& years deciphering falsehoods
Oh, the difference between posts about healing
& what it actually takes to heal...

Be Kind To Yourself
Vincent J. Hall II

Be kind to yourself
in the moments when
it's difficult.

Be kind to yourself
by staying in bed a
little longer today.

Be kind to yourself
by buying the cup of
coffee, even when you
shouldn't.

Be kind to yourself
by putting your phone
down & not doom scrolling.

Be kind to yourself
by watching that show
you've been putting off.

Be kind to yourself
by having another piece
of chocolate & another
glass of wine.

Be kind to yourself
and maybe take
the day off:

Go to a museum,
buy a book, stop &

get ice cream on
your way home.

No matter how you
do it. Be kind to
yourself.

Stone & Honey
Azure Hall

I loved the way you loved me, tender & removed. The smooth pieces of me that you claimed, rearranged, & presented to me in praises looked like a girl I used to know.

I loved that honey-sweet girl shining in your eyes. Reduced, refined, & familiar. She was so soft that I knew I could rest there for a while.

I loved the way you loved me as you led me by the hand through the shallows of my soul. Stopping to sit on the shoreline, you fell asleep fully clothed with your boots still on before the tide came in.

There with you, I dared not cast my eyes upon my own reflection; lest the terrible, writhing monster I'd become turn me to stone. I peeked at the creature from the safety of that beach, through the mirrors of your glasses, as the eels swam circles around my feet. They curled around the jagged edges left over after I carved myself from clay, chisel still gripped in my fingers.

The ribs I formed by hand looked to you like your own.

I loved the way you loved me as you passed my power back to me in kind words & kisses. But in your gradual generosity, the gorgon grew hungry. The coiled vipers of my canyons rose to claim what was never yours to give. You offered my self back to me and I received my glory as a gift, crediting you for the life-giving light of my own sun.

But they refused. & in their taking, light found light. Your river rock nymph glimpsed her likeness in the sea while you slept, serpents still locked around her ankles. Her eyes sought out shining sharp corners & happily found them.

What you so kindly returned to me once you were finished writing my story fused to its host like socket & bone. The sound of my divine reconstruction drowned out your drowsy-sweet nothings like a single shout into the cave.

Like found like, & gone was the fear of being turned to stone. Returned was the dangerous knowledge that I am of the stone. I created the stone. I molded the stone.

The masonry of stone on stone and light on self-illuminating light built my gaze & raised me above the crest of your eye line, revealing to me as you slept all that I forgot how to see.

Photosynthesis
Lianne Quintero

The pain was soil, for the seeds I planted needed dirt. Depth. Darkness.
To bloom.
To spread.
To infect & contaminate everything with this urging, need, desire, to
be.
To grow.
To revolutionize.
Pain was the soil that fertilized the path & allowed the birthing of this
womban
to *r i s e.*
It seeped through the cracks & crevices,
contaminated my very being,
ripped me apart until I could no longer ignore her throbbing.
To be raw,
open.
Pain,
you've been my greatest teacher.
My greatest enemy.
Greatest friend.
May we thank you,
for you are often numbed,
rejected,
&
not enough seen, accepted
& loved.
Thank you, soil, for creating the environment needed to be, this
today.

Departing
Kachay A. Bell

There's pain
that comes with
letting you go.
In order
to love myself though,
I had to cut the strings
from my heart
to your being
& finally embark
on my new journey
of loving me
& being content
with just me.

In Stillness
M. Watkins

In the stillness of the milky morn,
quiet is healing; to my spirit, I am borne.
Let the silence of still fill my empty cup.
To my inner voice, let my ears prick up.
Let me sit alone with myself as my first friend,
as my true friend.
As the one who values my truth, speaks my
truth, & walks my truth with me.
Let me caress myself with pure unconditional
love, unconditional acceptance.
Let me be the first to offer a hand when I
stumble & a shoulder when I cry.
If I love myself first, then others I can
love. If I am never there for me, then I
am never really there for any.

Untitled
Renee Lynn Furlow

Life can be so messy
with lines crossed daily.
For so long, I believed
if this happened,
then that would happen
& it became almost a running joke
because there was unwillingness
to commit to actual change.
I've come to the conclusion
I don't need a pile of *if,*
I deserve a pile of *when.*

Finding Happiness Within
Pooja Gudka

The misery was overwhelming
& the darkness
overpowering,
but slowly, I saw the light.
Instead of hate,
I chose love,
I chose happiness,
I chose me.

Push
Diana Kurniawan

When midnight strikes,
there is no glass slippers.
I tread on barefoot,
on hot coals of refuge.

Soles soft as cotton,
the coals burns me.
Terrors no longer shook.
Push through the damns.

Momentary terrors slips
in between my days.
Life cradles unexpected
sins of regrets and loss.

Travel through time
with no umbrella.
Only faith & prayer
Push through the grief.

Keep constant hope.
Object negative talk.
One fall leads to crippling
years of mysterious dreams.

Not everything works
to benefit my soul;
Solomon is company.
Push through the failures.

Steadfast grit leading,
better than sloth;

no excuse if bleeding,
pressure needs breathing.

Meditate on success.
No need to brag.
Shred bad visions.
Push through; work it.

My Missing Piece
Kachay A. Bell

All my life
I've been searching
for something
to fill in the cracks.
To feel complete.
Not knowing that
the only thing that can do so
is *me.*
I can only make myself
feel full & complete.
I only need me.

Norwich In July
Cara Morgan

I don't normally smoke sativa, but I am today.
Holding a joint out the window,
peering around the corner for sight of my neighbors. Relaxing when I
remember that the critters will let me know if someone's coming.
The squirrels
on the balcony next to ours have outsmarted the zip ties keeping them
out of the good seed. Chipmunks feast on what they drop & take
their prize to the safety of a nearby bush. An especially round tufted
titmouse eats the flesh of a cucumber I left them last night, the empty
skin a lonely ring on the ground. A resident pair of mourning doves
claim a branch on the treeline, watching like proud parents.
The sunrise is punctuated by their coos. They don't mind me
watching, because, to them, I'm part of it. If I stood here til
nightfall, I could watch Orion appear by
the big beech tree.

The cats have breakfast in their designated places
with their preferred texture
of wet food. Chunks, shreds & minced.
Gus snakes my legs, dropping his
favorite toy between my feet. A fish taco that crinkles.
His gesture says
throw it please. I do, of course.

I water the vegetables & flowers, trimming some meadow sage for my
kitchen. The peppers have sent out their first true leaves & the carrot
seedlings now look like carrot tops. I curse the aphids living in my
petunias, & greet the daddy long legs I've named Paul who eats them.
My hands smell like neem oil,
wet dirt & a trace of sativa smoke.

The cats are fed & so are the carrots, so the morning is mine.

Yesterday's coffee
left a ring on my desk that I replace with today's cup. I stretch my
body
& ask what it needs. Meditate an answer. Pull a tarot card to see what
the deck
thinks. Write a poem about it. Find myself at the window again,
breathing in the fresh air, watching the leaves dance around each
other in the breeze. Out back by the
treeline, life is happening painlessly. A squirrel cools its belly on a
branch.
Cellophane bees rest on the edge of a birdbath for a drink before
harvesting more nectar from my catnip. Nothing is out of place, not
even
me. Wildflowers bloom & stretch to the sun. Native ferns, grasses &
weeds.
Surviving, thriving. The forest's abundant green an oasis from the rest
of the
world. Peaceful in the shade of
the big beech tree.

In Gold
John Queor

Whenever I feel beige,
I wrap myself in gold sheets.
Despite the sky going black,
I shine like a star
until the sun returns.

It's okay
to be your own lullaby,
to sing yourself to sleep,
to dance on the clouds
while searching for peace.

Even when I feel hopeless,
I cover myself in gold beams.
I tuck myself into the soil
& patiently wait for the rain
to nourish me into bloom.

Thrive

Leigh Anne Hanigan

Trust in the wandering of your
heart & mind & inhale the scent of promise.
Realize what you want & need.
Imagine holding space for yourself to
validate the truth deep within.
Excavate your true nature & embrace who you are.

Kiss In The Hospital Courtyard
Jordan Merenick

A flower petal burning
      between mascots
of concrete

         between the hinges
of old age.

Nobody wins this war.
       At best,
it's a rearguard action,
but that doesn't mean
you shouldn't try
here
       on your coffee break
from the dentist.

Sweet Softness
Julia Yee

Surround yourself
with the soft & gentle:
fresh linen sheets enveloping you
on a purple spring night,
sun warmed waves washing over you
before melting into sunset,
sweet summer air caressing you
as you twirl in the twilight,
your own thoughts washed
& tumble dried
so that they are lighter and more comforting
than ever before.

June 1st
A. J. Flora

I rise from the grasp of sleep
& what greets me when I rise?
An old friend
gone for so long, it seems,
reaching through the cracks of my blinds,
stroking my face as if to tell me,
it's time, love,
it's okay,
& she laces up my shoes,
helps me down the stairs
& it's hard.
I open the door & pull some fruit out.
I cut it up & put it in a little container
as methodically & logically as I can
while she holds me from behind,
whispering words of encouragement.
She grew this to nourish me.
She grew this to help me succeed, thrive, live,
& with this, I put it in my bag because
she grew this because she loves me,
& with this, I march towards the door
step by step,
bite by bite,
day by day.
She kisses me when i open it,
good morning, I love you

I love you too,
day by day.

They Do Not Love You
J. Daniel Cruz

They do not love your voice,
for they silence it into the void.
They do not love your embrace,
for they keep you at arm's length.

They do not love your heart,
for they betray it & break it in half.
They do not love your skin,
for they paint & label over it.

They do not love your eyes,
for they deny the truth that filters inside.

They do not love you.

Only you can love you.

Who Am I?
A. R. Harlow

Who am I?
The question lingers.
For the time, unanswered.

What do I believe?
People try to say
those answers for me.

What do I want to be?
I'm told to get dreams
that make money.

Where is my core?
In acts of kindness
& unsteady gestures.
For hurting hearts,
lonely souls.
Peace, change, love,
all from me overflow.

A mother. A writer.
An artist. A visionary.
A student. A psychology major.

But does that list define the real me?
A world-changer, a risk-taker.
Enigmatic, I am a sojourner in this world.
My purpose, to weave poetry & prose, turning shapeless,
fathomless thoughts & forming them into unseen worlds.

But does that list define the real me?
Truth is found within the list,

but the lines are filled
with pretty titles.
Those do no justice
for what defines the person deep down inside.

Where is my core?
In helping others,
shedding a light & being the guiding eyes.
Changing the world
& changing lives,
aach one day at a time.

What do I want to be?
An inspiration to all the little children.
A role model for those young & old.
Rays of hope in a world of dark.
The person who leaves people longing for more of my heart.

What do I believe?
That even the smallest stone
can make the biggest difference.
Peace is possible in spite of all the hate
& love triumphs always.

Who am I?
I am a dreamer of a brighter future.
A paver of the pathway to a new light.
Enigmatic tendencies can shift the weight,
if only more people valued them;
enigmas, visionaries, introverts, the wise
will open everyone's eyes.

Who am I?
I am me, & that's okay.
I do me the best possible way.

Choosing Myself
Pooja Gudka

The little things
we do for ourselves
are what keep us together.
You see me taking a bath;
I see myself allowing me to relax.
You see me wearing makeup;
I see myself as a canvas
I painted with love.
You see my tattoos,
but I see a work of art.
You see a selfish being;
I see someone that cherishes themselves.

You, Dear
Kendall Hope

Darling,
you did your most
& now it is time to raise a toast
to the girl you once were,
still are,
& always will be.

It is *you,* dear.

You Do Not Have To Be Good
Cara Morgan

You do not have to be good.
You do not have to have perfected surfing the raging sea of yourself.
It's okay.
You do not need to defeat the ocean today.
You don't even have to leave your bed.
You do need to breathe & beat your heart & nourish your body.
Think of tomorrow, when the tide goes out.
Think of all the sea glass you'll find.
Pretty little things tumbled over and over,
not what they once were but beautiful all the same.
You do not have to be good,
but you do have to *be*.
If only to witness the next sunrise, the next heartbreak, the next thing
that makes you
feel alive.
This thing we call life is a series of mistakes & happy accidents.
& while I wish you every joy you can find,
it does not have to be good or easy or whole to be beautiful.

Heavenly Stretch Mark Blessed
Annie Vazquez

Some of us women
have been
heavenly stretch mark blessed.
We've been painted by the angels
& anointed
with ethereal lines
that glisten & sparkle
in hues of silver & white
across our bodies
like constellations.

Heavenly stretch mark blessed.
Oh yes, we have these
sacred gifts emblazoned on us

for a lifetime.
Divine tattoos dancing along our skin,
reminding us to celebrate & honor
how much our bodies do for us.
How much our bodies heal for us.
How much our bodies fight for us just to
grow, expand, glitter
& exist
heavenly stretch marked blessed.

Your Body Is Your Homeland
Julia Yee

Find the hollows that bloom within you—
the places of rest, of pause, of power.
Seek out that rare stillness in the spaces
between your bones, amidst the jumble
of your joints. Curl up & stay there a while.

Garden Of Worthiness

Nicole Smith

The Garden of Worthiness
exudes peace.
Unless there's a party,
then it's strictly 90's hip hop & r&b.
The garden is filled with flowers.
The perfume in the air is self-love.
I healing my wounds one by one,
by handling my inner child softly, with kid gloves.
There's tranquility all around me.
Finally, a calmness settled within.
I am worthy of love just as I am.
A new chapter of my life now begins.

Aesthetic Sincerity
Taya Boyles

A soul is as living as a bleeding heart,
as desperate for care & attention
as an infant that hungers.
Those lifetime pangs
lead the toddler to the cookie jar.
You can't wait until the first frost to install insulation;
even a draft allows
the coldness to spread to the
rest of the house. We're all hands & eyes
grasping through an Alaskan storm,
sporadic & cataclysmic into what is known.

Repair what is broken by the roots-up
before the lights flicker,
before the day's light & darkness
bleed into one another,
before spring ceases
to exist in winter's grip.

Trust The Process
Tim Hall

When the day looks impossible,
the couch feels comfortable & sunrays splashing
from the bay windows look
uneventful,
trust the process.
When a conversation with your partner seems
daunting & your feelings eat away at
your tongues ability to produce words,
trust the process.
When depression is the dust that refuses to be swept from the floor
& all you want is
freedom from having to clean up the destructive thoughts that fall,
trust the process.
When song doesn't sound as beautiful
& melody no longer scales your arms with goosebumps,
trust the process.
When fear resembles the worn notebook in your book bag,
the rarely opened Evernote app on your phone,
or the twice folded post-it notes dusting your desk
that stare & stare & hover &
wait & tire & toggle & get misplaced & are found & still not touched,
trust the process.

1. You are tired & the couch is still warm
from the imprint of your back.
The outside taunts you to smile in its direction.
Close your beautiful eyes & feel the heat wash your tired away.
2. Your feelings matter & your words hold value, use them.
It is impossible for your partner to know
the lining of your mind or heart or hurt.
3. When the dust settles you will still be a person.
All pumping blood, moving limbs &

processing mind. Press your quaking hand
against the valley of your chest,
the home where your survival lives,
the carrier of your liberation.
4. Sound waves need not an ear to be heard
nor a piece of skin to scare. Listen to the
silence of your beautiful body
& welcome the music in your story.
5. Trust the process of your healing.
Trust the process of your hope.
Trust the process of your deliverance.
Trust the process of your mindfulness.
Trust the process of your pen.

The Orchard
Flor Ana

My feet are planted on the ground,
rooted in my being.
But my branches
are reaching the stars,
extending across the cosmos.

Like wind brushing against the heat of summer,
my growth is coming
s l o w l y,
little by little,
lesson by lesson.

My growth is coming in
bouts of heaven-kissed raindrops, in
sprinklings of bloom.

Suddenly, I know.
I am a tree
becoming an orchard.
I am a being
becoming the universe.
I am
growing into myself,
into my element,
one soft petal,
one fallen leaf
at
a
time,
ready for my *primavera*.

THE POETS

Aphrodite's Devotee is a poet, intuitive tarot reader, and Reiki Master from Florida. She has been writing poetry since she was 15, and with her spiritual journey, her work has evolved into a collection of poems meant to tap into the soul's inner dialogue. She believes that poetry and the creative arts in general are capable of healing people deeply. *Glow: Self-Care Poetry for the Soul* is her poetry publication debut.
Instagram: @aphroditesdevotee444

Tiffiny Rose Allen is a writer, creator, and poet originally from the state of Florida. She began writing at an early age and self-published her first collection of poetry Leave The Dreaming To The Flowers in 2017. With four more poetry collections and a collection of short stories, Tiffiny curated their own anthology in 2022 titled Dreams In Hiding, and in 2023 published their sixth poetry collection, At The Beginning of Yesterday, with Indie Earth Publishing. When she is not writing, she is working on anything that excites her.
Instagram: @dreamsinhiding.writing

Bushra Ali is a poet and writer from Pakistan. Born and raised in Karachi, she's been living in this enthralling world of writing since her childhood. The spark of storytelling and dancing with words was ignited in heart by the countless books she read in her school library. She believes in the saying that 'Everyone has a story to tell,' and she chooses to write her stories and others by her words. She couldn't make her way here if not for the perpetual love and support of her loving family, wonderful friends, and amazing teachers. A little self-effacing girl at heart, Bushra showcased her writings mainly through social media platforms and then made her way to a few magazines. She has a passionate love for literature and all that holds. Bushra aspires to publish her own books someday. *Glow: Self-Care Poetry for the Soul* is her first anthology.
Instagram: @calm_pace

Flor Ana is a Cuban-American writer, poet, and musician who made her literary debut with her self-published poetry collection, *Perspective (and other poems)*. Since then, Flor has released various poetry collections including *The Language of Fungi & Flowers*, *Nourish Your Temple: Self-Love & Care Poetry*, and *A Moth Fell In Love With The Moon*. Flor has also been featured in various poetry anthologies and has released spoken word poetry on all streaming platforms. She also enjoys doing on-the-spot typewritten poetry at events and markets.
Instagram: @littleearthflower

Jade Baas is a twenty-year-old Filipino artist from Daly City, California. She extends her creative perspective through poetry, capturing photos, and combining digital and mixed media art. She soon will start her music and entrepreneur journey, as well. Jade's intention is for her art to become meditation to others, to awaken one's higher consciousness and ascend oneself into a healed awakening.
Instagram: @jxd3.poetry

Kachay A. Bell is a poetess from New York City and has been writing since her school days. When she is not writing poetry, she finds herself captivated with mystery/thriller and romance novels with the latter being one of the topics featured in her writings. She also loves quality time spent with the ones she loves, pouring her heart out, appreciating the beauty that comes with life and hopes to one day have her own published poetry collection.
Instagram: @poetrybykachay

Taya Boyles is a writer based in Richmond, Virginia, and as a senior at Virginia Commonwealth University, she is currently pursuing a Bachelor of Arts in English. Taya's writing journey started when she was published at just eight years old, and has come a long way from misspelling glue. Since then, her poetry and flash fiction has appeared in literary magazines such as Split Lip Magazine,

Vermillion, Pwatem, Hot Pot Magazine, and more.
Instagram: @tayatheauthor

Cortney Casey lives in Auburn Hills, Michigan, and Miami, Florida, with her husband and rescue chihuahua, Brida. She attended the University of Michigan and worked as a reporter at a community newspaper chain for more than eleven years before leaving to launch a small business. Cortney recently completed her first novel, with a second in progress. *Glow: Self-Care Poetry for the Soul* is her poetry publication debut.
Instagram: @cortbythepage

Renzo Del Castillo was born in Lima, Peru, in 1983, and was educated at the University of Florida, leaving with a B.A. in English, specializing in Victorian Literature, and an M.A. in Mass Communications, specializing in Intercultural Communications. Renzo currently resides in Miami, but he prioritizes traveling in order to experience and be exposed to the tenets of other cultures. He strongly believes that it is through art that we find the divinity of truth, the pathway of communication with others; that through this connection we are made whole. While he has spent the last 10 years as an executive in the healthcare industry, Renzo has been previously published in literary publications such as Literary Yard, the Acentos Review, the Scarlet Leaf Review, and the Ekphrastic Review. His debut poetry collection *Still* releases in the fall of 2023.
Instagram: @elrenz

A. J. Flora is a poet and musician from Raleigh, NC. He is currently pursuing an undergraduate degree in Psychology from UNC Chapel Hill. He is an advocate for animal rights and the rights of minorities in the American South.
Instagram: @ajflora.jpg

Courtney Force is a mystic poet and spiritual guide. Her poetry is influenced by spiritual experiences and by her interest in psycholo-

gy, nature, the cosmos, and human emotions. Courtney endeavors to create healing, connection, beauty, and remembrance through her writing. *Soul Dancer*, her debut poetry collection, was released on June 30, 2022. A lover of travel and adventures, Courtney currently splits her time between California and England.
Instagram: @courtneyforcefield

dsb.poetry is the brainchild of Matt Nickles; a watered down, modern day, "dollar store" version of Charles Bukowski. Most of his writing is strongly influenced by writers of the beat generation, his home state of Pennsylvania, and the experiences he's had throughout his life. Though he loved to write fiction as a child, Matt picked up poetry in his early twenties as a way to pass the time during a difficult period in his life. Since then, he has found comfort in the art and has held it close ever since. His debut poetry chapbook, *We Were Fire in the Night*, releases July 11, 2023.
Instagram: @dsb.poetry

Renee Lynn Furlow is a seasoned writer and offers spiritually-based services as the "Unique-tivity Guide." She owns "Catch A Falling Star" and has plans for content on a new blog coming soon. Currently, she has two short eBooks available on Amazon, Defining Love Worth Catching and Itty Bitty Book - Rose Quartz, with more planned. She is currently writing her poetic memoir, Beauty In the Breakdown, due out September, 2023.
Instagram: @reneelynn_0

Vanessa 'Kaylyn Marie' Gallegos resides in Denver, Colorado, is on the cusp of her thirties and spends her time making art, doing runway shows, and acting while supporting her community. Poetry has always been a way to express her feelings and life experiences and she utilizes this to connect with those who are unable to put their own feelings into words.
Instagram: @a rt_by.ness

Pooja Gudka is an aspiring writer, blogger and freelancer currently working from Kenya. Her journey began as a blogger when she created her multi-niche blog, Lifesfinewhine, as a teenager to share her experiences with life, mental health, travel and more. Since then, her blog has grown and is now her full-time passion. Her writing has been published in books like *Hidden In Childhood: A Poetry Anthology* as well as multiple magazines.
Instagram: @herbivoreonajourney

Azure Hall is a poet and essayist from Virginia. She studied English Literature at the College of William and Mary where her essay, "Finding My Mother," received the 2016 Tiberius Gracchus Jones Prize for Nonfiction. She is a passionate conservationist and her writing is heavily influenced by her relationship with the natural world. She lives in Cheyenne, Wyoming, with her daughter, Zooey, and their cat, Valentine.
Instagram: @azure_hall_author

Vincent J. Hall II is a New Jersey-based writer who made his literary debut with *The Drinks Between Us*. A History graduate from William Paterson University, Vincent helps lead ArtPride New Jersey Foundation's advocacy and governmental affairs efforts. When he is not helping his community and advocating for arts and culture, Vincent enjoys attending Phillies games with his partner, Megan, going to museums, and spending time with friends.
Instagram: @vincevangoah

Leigh Anne Hanigan lives in Hunterdon County, NJ and is mom to three independent daughters and two dependent dogs! She is passionate about the outdoors, exercise, music, photography and of course, writing. She has taught at the elementary level for twenty-five years and is currently running adult workshops in poetry and journaling. You can read some of Leigh Anne's writing at www.journey-blog.com.
Instagram: @journeyinward13

Johanna Hatch is a poet writing at the intersection of nature, kinship, and magic. A native of Cape Cod, MA, she now lives in Wisconsin with her family. Her poetry has also been featured in the anthology *The Spell Jar: Poetry for the Modern Witch*.
Instagram: @johannajanet

Amelie Honeysuckle is a student at the University of Colorado Boulder who loves spending her time meandering through her local trails on bike and foot. Amelie is a lover of words and believes that one of the most beautiful ways to colorfully create is through the art of words. Amelie loves finding unconventional beauty in her environment, thrives through writing love poetry for her people, and is a believer that "you make your own happiness." *What Once Was An Inside Out Rainbow* is her debut poetry collection that released April 2023.
Instagram: @wordsbyamelie

Kendall Hope is a Colorado native, who thrives off of sunshine and has been a creative since the time she was small. She loves exploring the outdoors and being a part of nature, which translates into her poetry. In 2022, she debuted as an author with her poetry collection *Pockets of Lavender* and has gone on to be featured in a variety of anthologies including *Unsent Love Letters: An Anthology of Words Left Unspoken*, *The Spell Jar: Poetry for the Modern Witch*, and *Glow: Self-Care Poetry for the Soul*. Kendall's works have also been featured in local stores in Colorado Springs, like Poor Richard's, Ivywild School, and Eclectic CO.
Instagram: @kendallhopepoetry

A. W. Jones is a poet and writer residing in the Pacific Northwest. A firm believer in the healing power of writing, she is currently working on her first poetry collection about healing from complex childhood trauma. Jones received her Bachelor of Arts in Psychology from California State University, Sacramento and is currently completing a Masters degree in Applied Behavior Analysis. *Glow:*

Self-Care Poetry for the Soul is Jones's literary debut.
Instagram: @awjones.poetry

Alshaad Kara is a Mauritian poet who writes from his heart. He won the Gal's Guide Anthology 2023 People's Choice Award for his poem Prelude, and his latest poems were published in two anthologies, *Gal's Guide Anthology: Journey* and *Suicide Vol.2*, two journals, *Literary Cognizance Vol. 111* and *Cultural Reverence Vol. V; No. 2, April 2023*, and one magazine, *Prodigy Magazine-February 2023*.
Instagram: @alshaad_kara

Diana Kurniawan is a poet and writer based in Berthoud, Colorado. Her inspirations comes from her healing journey, the good people she meets and life experiences. Prior to poetry and fiction writing, she was a content writer and journalist in the Denver areas. Find her at www.DianaKurniawan.com.
Instagram: @dianakurniawanwrites

Jaime Lam is a queer, biracial tea fanatic. Graduated from Knox College, she majored in English and Creative Writing. She tends to lean towards poetry, essays, and the wilder card of urban fantasy. Originally, Jaime is from the corn part of Illinois, but is currently admiring the moss in Savannah, GA. As a person, she has a habit of laughing ridiculously hard at her own jokes, makes too big of a deal of someone's birthday, and wants to personally remind you to drink water. Her work can be found in Viewless Wings, Breakbread Lit, Papers Publishing, and Sandhills Literary.
Instagram: @rainjmerain

Ashley Lilly is a queer, African American poet from New York. Their writing has been featured in Footnotes by The Poetry Project, the Black Poppy Review and the *Inspirations* anthology. Ashley has self-published several poetry books, including *Wanderer* and *Young Heart,* as well as a collection of short stories titled

Impossible Things. Ashley holds a bachelor's degree in English from LIU Post. To read more of their work, visit AshleyLillyBlog. WordPress.com.
Instagram: @ashleylillyx3

Jordan Merenick is an author and poet from Pittsburgh, PA. He has been published by Lightning Tower Press, On-The-High Literary Magazine ,Clove & White, Calla Press, Nitrogen House & Rune. He loves spending time with his family when not writing.
Instagram: @jordanmerenickwrites

Nicole Menzzasalma is a poet, librarian, yogi, and mama of two boys. After three decades of writing poetry, destiny led her to collaborate on *Glow: Self-Care Poetry for the Soul*. Nicole has a MLIS from Queens College, a BA in Creative Writing from Hofstra University, and a 500-hour Yoga Teacher certification.
Instagram: @menzthepoet

Cara Morgan is a nonbinary, queer, disabled, and neurodivergent poet and artist from Exeter, Maine. They host a Spotify podcast called the sunshine lounge and virtual poetry workshops for traditionally marginalized voices to make art. They are super passionate about their cats, cool rocks, making playlists, funky earrings, and the color yellow.
Instagram: @caramorganpoet

Thuy ("twee") Nguyen is the poet, writer, speaker, creative, and founder of The Twiggy Mother—imparting her insights to inspire others to live soulfully empowered. An artist at heart, she found herself painting with words to make beautiful nonsense of her life and lives to beautify the world around her. She is a mother of three in the Colorado Rockies, who are her inspirational forces to instill deep roots for the future generation.
Instagram: @thetwiggymotherwriter

Jake Price is a sophomore student who spends too much time reading his poetry to his cat, who has yet to give him any useful feedback. He was born in Texas, but now resides in McConnelsburg, Pennsylvania. Writing has been something he has loved doing ever since he was a little kid, and he hopes to one day make a living off of it. His poetry has been published in Rivercraft Magazine, Cream Scene Carnival, and The Poet Magazine.
Instagram: @nolenprice

John Queor is a queer poet, scribbling most of his work while cloaked in the early morning darkness. John resides in central New York, but one day hopes to live in Maine, in a small cottage by the sea. He debuted as a poet with his first collection of poetry, *Burnt Lavender*, and has since published his second collection *Resembling A Moth*, and has been featured in a variety of anthologies including *The Spell Jar: Poetry for the Modern Witch* and *Dreams in Hiding: An Amalgamation of Verses and Prose.*
Instagram: @johnnyqu33r

Lianna Quintero is a twenty-six-year-old queer woman, who currently resides in Miami, Florida and is a full-time yoga instructor. Lianne is a multifaceted woman who also loves to write. Her pieces consist of erotic poetry and the dynamics of divine masculine and feminine energies. She made her publishing debut in the anthology *The Spell Jar: Poetry for the Modern Witch.*
Instagram: @_lillsss

Kristen Noelle Richards is a poet based in Colorado Springs currently working towards a BA in Creative Writing at Colorado College. Kristen writes about the natural world intertwined with the mind-body connection, drawing upon her own experiences in the mountains and desert. She loves creating poetry outdoors, usually accompanied by the sunrise, an oat milk latte, and Mary Oliver's poem *Wild Geese*. Her debut poetry collection, *as if to return myself to the sea*, releases August 8th, 2023.

Instagram: @kristenrichardspoetry

Nicole Smith is an advocate for mental health and body acceptance. She lives just outside of Pittsburgh with her husband and daughters. Recently she was published in the Pennsylvania Bards Western PA Poetry Review 2023. If Nicole isn't writing poetry, you can find her with her nose in a book.
Instagram: @momshorts80

Veronica Szymankiewicz is a Cuban-American poet born and raised in Miami, Florida. Her work has been published in numerous anthologies. Veronica pursued a doctoral degree in Clinical Psychology, acquiring a Master's degree along the way. With five classes left, she pivoted into a career as an elementary school teacher. Her writing is as eclectic as she is and includes various genres and themes including mental health, trauma, narcissistic abuse, love, heartbreak, the metaphysical, dark poetry, as well as inspirational work. She is a mental health advocate, narcissistic abuse survivor, a lifelong writer, and lover of words. She considers poetry to be a cathartic outlet. Veronica writes as a way to heal herself, with hopes that her words will resonate with others, healing them along the way as well.
Instagram: @verorisingpoetry

Cece Rose Trezza is a writer, poet, tattoo artist, freestyler, and singer living in sunny Los Angeles. Their work focuses on cultivating self love and finding ways to work with the darkness, rather than against. They love to combine elements of spirituality and comedy in all that they create. Their debut was their poem "Luna" featured in *The Spell Jar: Poetry for the Modern Witch*.
*Instagram: @cece_hehe_*

Annie Vazquez is a poet, writer, and former freelance journalist featured in the Miami Herald, Refinery29, NBC6, and Vogue. Her blog, The Fashion Poet, is Miami's #1 lifestyle blog and her

wellness brand, Annie the Alchemist, has been featured on People Magazine, Man Repellar, and Time Out Magazine. Annie has published ebooks on self-love and wellness, and has released an affirmation deck titled *Affirmations for Abundance*. Her poetry has been featured in anthologies including *The Spell Jar: Poetry for the Modern Witch* and *Love Letters to the 305*. Her debut poetry collection will be released in 2023.
Instagram: @anniewriteswords

M. Watkins is a spiritual eclectic writer, artist and poet who resides in the state of Georgia, though she really believes we all are natives of somewhere else.
Instagram: @thebtfgazette

Kelli Weldon was born and raised in Louisiana and now resides in Texas. She studied journalism and literature at Northwestern State University in Natchitoches, Louisiana, and served on the editorial board of its literary magazine, Argus. Find her poetry in publications including Frost Meadow Review, Eclectica Magazine, Duck Duck Mongoose Magazine, Rewrite The Stars Review, and Boats Against The Current.
Instagram: @kelliwritespoems

Julia Yee is a poet and writer who recently moved from New York City to Paris to follow her dreams of creating a life dedicated to literature, art, and all things sublime. When she's not posting original poetry on her Instagram page, she writes YA fantasy, works at a local bookstore, and co-hosts a book-themed podcast, Meet Me At The Bookstore. Her work has been featured online with Glass Gates Publishing, In Her Space Magazine, and in the *Daydreams and Lost Wishes Poetry Anthology* by Poetic Reveries. She is also currently working on her own debut poetry collection, to be release in late 2023.
Instagram: @day.dream.diaries

About The Publisher

Indie Earth Publishing is an author-first, independent publishing company based in Miami, FL, dedicated to giving artists and writers the creative freedom they deserve in publishing their poetry, fiction, and short stories. We provide our authors a plethora of services that are meant to make them feel like they are finally releasing the book of their dreams, including professional editing, design, formatting, organization, advanced reader teams, and so much more. With Indie Earth Publishing, you're more than just another author, you're part of the Indie Earth creative family, making a difference in the world, one book at a time.

www.indieearthbooks.com

For inquiries, please email:
indieearthpublishinghouse@gmail.com

Instagram: @indieearthbooks